Pursuing Basic Steps to Discipleship

www.GoodSoil.com/Resources

The Way to Joy—Kids: Pursuing Basic Steps to Discipleship

Association of Baptists for World Evangelism
P.O. Box 8585
Harrisburg, PA 17105 USA

980 Adelaide Street South, Suite 34
London, Ontario N6E 1R3 CANADA

Editors and Content Developers: Wayne Haston, Ron Berrus & Karen Weitzel
Concept Developers: ABWE's Essential Mission Components Training Team

Cover and Interior Graphic Design: Miriam Miller Design
Custom Photography: Jeff Raymond, Miriam Miller Design
Stock Photography: 123rf.com

Phone: (877) 959-2293

Library of Congress Cataloging-in-Publications Data (application pending)

The Way to Joy—Kids: Pursuing Basic Steps to Discipleship
ISBN 978-1-888796-86-5

Printed in the United States of America.

Email: Info@GoodSoil.com
Web: www.GoodSoil.com

Contents

Our Bible Study Agreement

This agreement should be signed below by the learner and the leader.

As the "learner" in this series of Bible lessons, I will:

- Read and answer the questions and memorize the Bible verse or verses that go with each lesson. I know there are extra Bible verses for *The Chronological Bridge to Life* in Lesson 2 that are optional.
- Read the Bible chapters in "My Bible Reading Plan and Prayer Journal" as indicated on pages 54 through 64.
- Do my best to be present and prompt for each Bible lesson.
- Pray for my Bible Study leader.

Signed ____

Date ________________

As the "leader" in this series of Bible lessons, I will:

- Be a good example by preparing myself thoroughly to lead each lesson. I will memorize all of the Bible verses assigned for each lesson, including those for *The Chronological Bridge to Life*.
- Read at least a chapter each day in my Bible.
- Do my best to be present and prompt for each Bible lesson.
- Pray for you as you seek to learn more about God's way to joy.

Signed ____

Date ________________

Introduction
for the Student

The Way to Joy—Kids is designed to help you become a committed follower of Jesus Christ.

The ten lessons in this book will introduce you to important teachings that will help you understand what God wants you to know from His Word and to follow each day.

In each lesson you will learn just basics of each topic. There is so much more to learn about these topics, so you are encouraged to continue to study them after completing *The Way to Joy—Kids*. As you do, you will learn even more about the Bible and what God wants you to do—and you will grow in your faith. You can ask an adult believer to help you learn more about God's Word. This process is called discipleship and means one person who believes the Bible helps another person learn more about the Bible.

Now, dig into God's wonderful Word that will lead you on *The Way to Joy!*

Instructions
for the Leader

- Review *The Way to Joy—Kids* book with the student and explain the work that will need to be done for each lesson.
- Explain the time required to complete the book. It is preferable to meet on a regular basis and cover one lesson each session.
- Use “Our Bible Study Agreement” on page 4 to encourage commitment to the study.
- Ask the student to read each lesson ahead of time and fill in the answers to the questions in his/her book.
- Point out the memory verse or verses for each lesson that is to be memorized. These verses appear at the end of the lesson. The goal for Bible memory is for both the leader and the student to recite all of the verses by the end of this lesson series.
- Lessons 1 and 2 both have six pages in order to cover necessary content. Lessons 3-10 each have four pages.
- Even though the student was asked to read through and complete the lesson prior to meeting with the leader, it is wise to go over the entire lesson with the student when the leader and student meet. This way the leader can determine if the student understands the content and, if not, can explain at that point anything that is not understood.
- Pray for—and with—your student.
- The Bible was originally written in Hebrew and Greek. Because most people do not read these languages, scholars who understood them translated the Bible into English (example: The King James Bible is one of these English Bible translations). The process of taking the Bible from one language and writing it in another is called translation and takes years because the scholars work hard to make sure the translation is accurate—the English (or other language) translation means just what the Hebrew Old Testament and Greek New Testament say. Today there are many translations of the Bible in English and in other languages. The Bible verses used in *The Way to Joy—Kids* come from the English Standard Version (ESV) Bible. You may use, and have your student(s) use, whichever accurate Bible translation you choose.

Additional Website Support and Resources can be found at: www.GoodSoil.com

- Free Leader’s Guide for using *The Way to Joy—Kids*
- Information about translations of *The Way to Joy—Kids*
- Additional evangelism and discipleship resources
- Online ordering

The Joy of Hope: 1

Knowing God's Eternal Plan Gives Us Hope

Important Facts to Know about the Bible

The Bible is one book that contains many books. There are 66 books in the Bible.

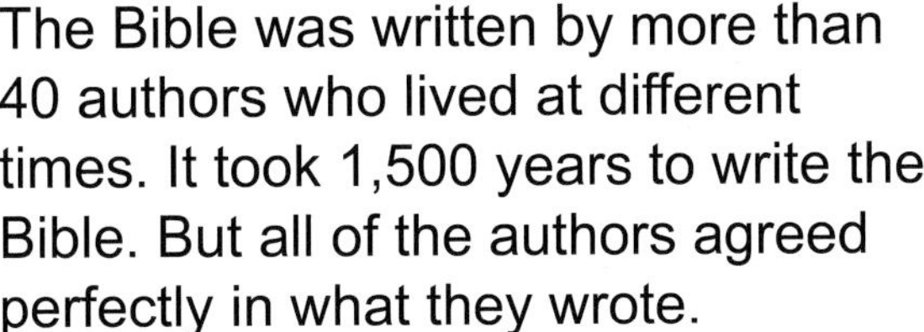

The Bible was written by more than 40 authors who lived at different times. It took 1,500 years to write the Bible. But all of the authors agreed perfectly in what they wrote.

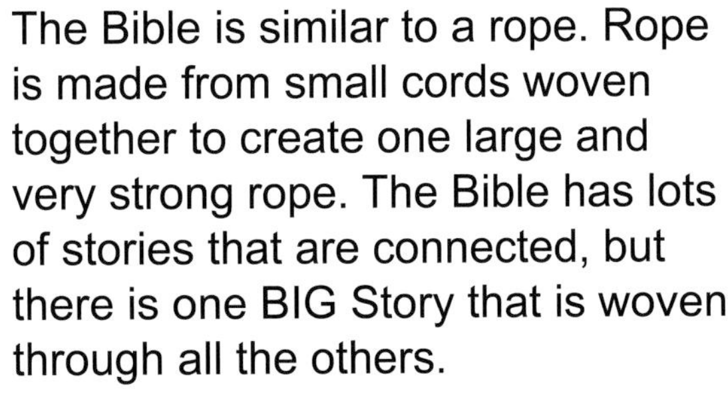

The Bible is similar to a rope. Rope is made from small cords woven together to create one large and very strong rope. The Bible has lots of stories that are connected, but there is one BIG Story that is woven through all the others.

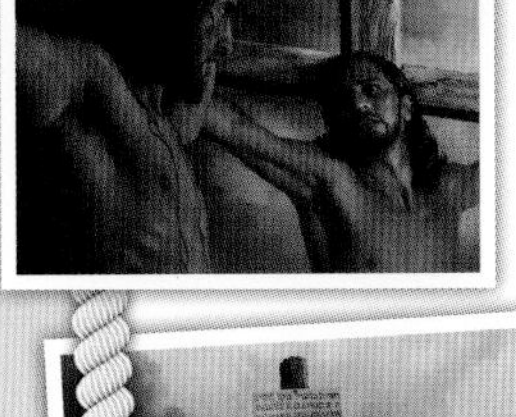
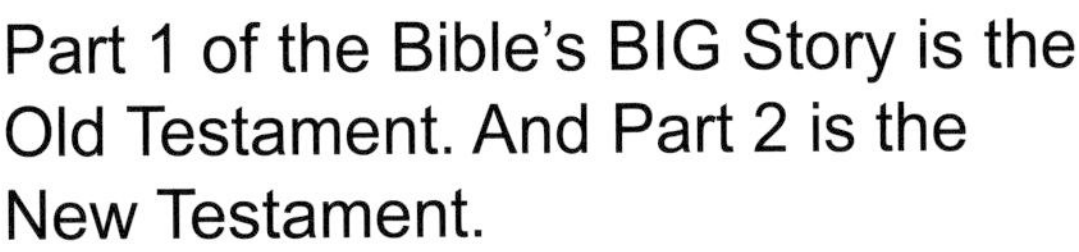

Part 1 of the Bible's BIG Story is the Old Testament. And Part 2 is the New Testament.

1

The Old Testament Is Part

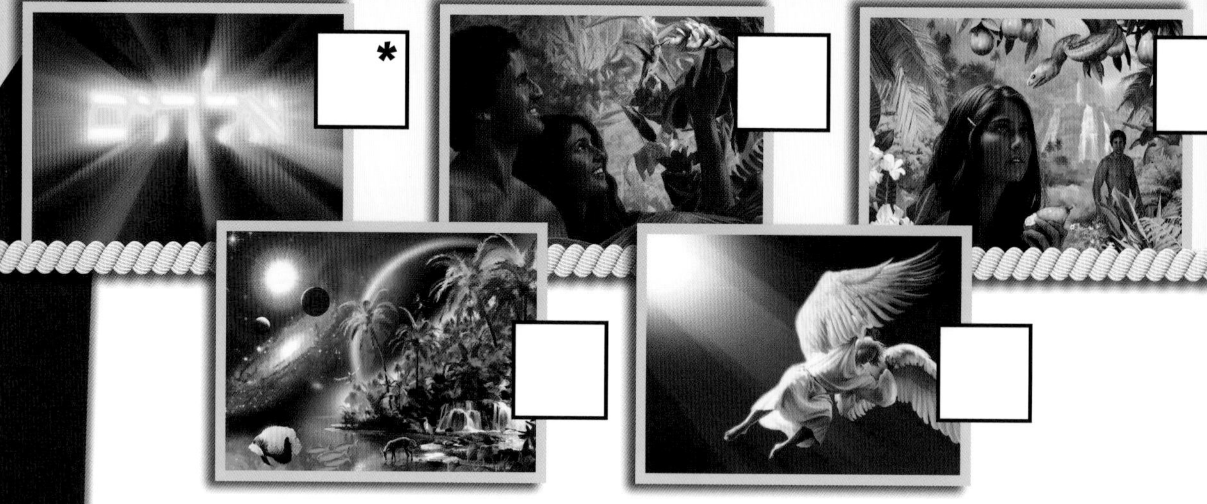

Match the statements below with the pictures above. Put the correct number in the box beside each picture.

1. The first sentence in the Bible tells us that there is a God and that He has always existed. **Genesis 1:1***

2. The Bible says that God created the universe, including our earth and its heavens. God also created plants and animals. **Genesis 1:1-25**

3. Then God created a man and a woman, Adam and Eve. God told them to rule over all the earth and not eat fruit from a certain tree. **Genesis 1:26-31; 2:7-25**

4. Lucifer had been a beautiful angel but led other angels to rebel against God. Lucifer became known as Satan, the Devil. **Ezekiel 28:11-17; Isaiah 14:12-15**

5. God loved Adam and Eve. He said, "Do not eat from the forbidden tree." Satan defied God and tempted Eve. She ate and caused Adam to eat. **Genesis 3:1-6**

*The word in this picture is the Hebrew word for "Elohim," a common name for God in the original Old Testament language.

n the Bible's BIG Story

6. God is holy and judges fairly. When Adam and Eve disobeyed, they immediately experienced the result of their sin: separation from God. **Genesis 3:7-13; 5:5**

7. God promised that one day a special descendant of Eve would defeat Satan. **Genesis 3:14-15**

8. Adam and Eve tried to cover their guilt and shame with fig leaves. God replaced the leaves with clothing He made from animal skins. **Genesis 3:7, 21**

9. God directed Moses to build a movable place for worship. There the Israelites offered sacrifices and received forgiveness of their sins. **Exodus 40:17-34; Leviticus 1:1-4, 10**

10. Throughout the Israelites' history, God inspired His prophets to tell details ahead of time about a special Israelite, King, and Savior who would be born at a future time.
Isaiah 7:14; 9:1-2, 6-7; 52:13—53:12

The Bible references (like "Genesis 1:1") tell us where in the Bible this information is found.

1 The New Testament Is Part 2

Match the statements below with the pictures above. Put the correct number in the box beside each picture.

11. At God's chosen time, He sent His Son to Earth. God's Son was born of a virgin named Mary. He would become the Special King and Savior that God had promised for centuries. **Matthew 1:1-2, 18-25; Luke 2:1-14**

12. God's prophet, John the Baptist, stated that Jesus of Nazareth was the Special King and Savior, God's Lamb, who would take away the sin of the world. **John 1:29-34**

13. One time, Jesus told an important religious leader that he must experience a spiritual birth in order to enter God's kingdom. **John 3:1-18**

14. Several times when Jesus declared that He was equal to and one with God, some people were greatly offended and tried to kill Him. **John 5:16-18; 8:48-59; 10:22-33**

15. Jesus died on a cross as the perfect sacrificial Lamb for sin. His death crushed Satan's head, just as God promised Adam and Eve. **Luke 23:26-38; 1 Corinthians 5:7**

in the Bible's BIG Story

16. As Jesus was dying, one guilty man, who was crucified beside Him put his faith in Jesus and received the gift of life in a place called "paradise" after he died. **Luke 23:39-47**

17. On the third day after Jesus died and was buried, God supernaturally raised Him from the dead to show His power over sin, death, and Hell. **Luke 24:1-12, 36-43**

18. After His resurrection, Jesus appeared many times to His disciples on earth. Then He ascended to Heaven to be with His Father. **1 Corinthians 15:3-8; Acts 1:6-11**

19. At the end of earthly time, unbelievers will stand in front of God to be sentenced to eternal punishment for their sins. **Revelation 20:11-15**

20. But God's Story ends with wonderful news. Everyone who has trusted Jesus as Savior will enter a beautiful paradise where there is no sin and they will live there eternally with God. **Revelation 21:1—22:5**

The Bible references (like "Matthew 1:1-2") tell us where in the Bible this information is found.

1

See How Well You Know the Bible's BIG Story

Go back to pages 8 and 9 and cover up the ten statements underneath the Bible event pictures. Just looking at the pictures, see how well you can tell the BIG Story of the Bible in the Old Testament.

1. **What parts of the Story in the Old Testament were the hardest for you to understand yourself or to tell clearly? Why?**

Now, go to pages 10 and 11 and do the same thing for the BIG Story of the Bible in the New Testament.

2. **What parts of the Story in the New Testament were the hardest for you to understand or to tell clearly? Why?**

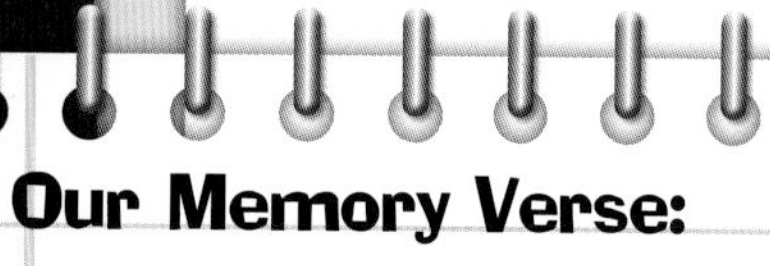

Our Memory Verse:
John 3:16

For God so loved the world, that he gave his only Son, that whoever believes in him should not perish but have eternal life.

Practice learning the verse by writing it below:

Reference:

Verse:

The Joy of Eternal Life: 2

Receiving God's Salvation Gives Us Eternal Life

Find the Meaning: Chronological

To arrange events in the order they happened, starting with the earliest/oldest event and ending with the most recent event.

The Chronological Bridge to Life

Contains Eight *Very* Important Bible Truths

This bridge is also called the "ChronoBridge"

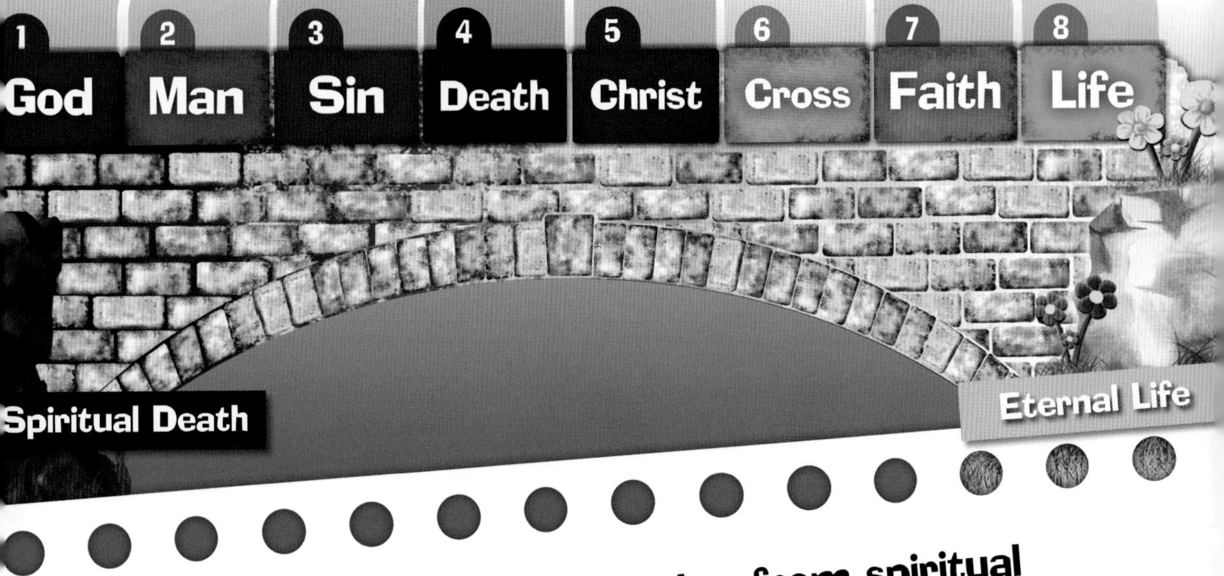

1 God
2 Man
3 Sin
4 Death
5 Christ
6 Cross
7 Faith
8 Life

Spiritual Death

Eternal Life

Why do you think this bridge from spiritual death to eternal life is called the Chronological Bridge to Life?

2

God

1

Hebrews 11:6

And without faith it is impossible to please him, for whoever would draw near to God must believe that he exists and that he rewards those who seek him.

1. **When you come to God, what is the first thing you must believe?**

2. **What is the second thing?**

My Faith Response:

I must believe God exists.He is the Creator and Judge. I am responsible for my actions and must answer for them to Him.

Man

2

Genesis 2:7

Then the Lord God formed the man of dust from the ground and breathed into his nostrils the breath of life, and the man became a living creature.

3. **Why must all people answer to God for their actions?**

My Faith Response:

I must believe that I am made by God. He loves me and I should obey Him all the time.

Sin

3

Romans 3:23

For all have sinned and fall short of the glory of God.

4. Why are all people sinners?

My Faith Response:

I must believe that I have sinned against our holy God and I deserve His punishment for my sin.

Death

4

Hebrews 9:27

And just as it is appointed for man to die once, and after that comes judgment.

5. What will happen to everyone after they die?

My Faith Response:

I must believe that I will die someday and be judged by God. I cannot escape this judgment on my own.

Christ

5

John 14:6

Jesus said to him, "I am the way, and the truth, and the life. No one comes to the Father except through me."

6. **How many true ways are there to God?**

My Faith Response:

I must believe that Jesus Christ is the sinless Son of God and is the only way to eternal life.

Cross

6

1 Peter 2:24

He himself bore our sins in his body on the tree, that we might die to sin and live to righteousness. By his wounds you have been healed.

7. **Explain: "He himself bore our sins in his body on the tree."**

My Faith Response:

I must believe that Jesus Christ, God's Son, died for my sins and rose from the dead to give me eternal life.

Faith

7

Ephesians 2:8-9

For by grace you have been saved through faith. And this is not your own doing; it is the gift of God, not a result of works, so that no one may boast.

8. **What must a person do to have the gift of God?**

My Faith Response:

I must realize that my good works will not save me, then completely trust that only Jesus Christ's death on the cross will save me.

Life

8

John 11:25-26

Jesus said to her, "I am the resurrection and the life. Whoever believes in me, though he die, yet shall he live, and everyone who lives and believes in me shall never die. Do you believe this?"

9. **What do the words "though he die, yet shall he live" mean?**

My Faith Response:

I must realize that Jesus has power over death and that He has promised eternal life to those who put their total trust in Him.

2

See How Well You Know the ChronoBridge

The Chronological Bridge to Life

From memory, try to write the ***eight very important Bible truths*** in the places on the bridge where they should be. Use the word bank if you need help and only look back at the previous pages if you have to.

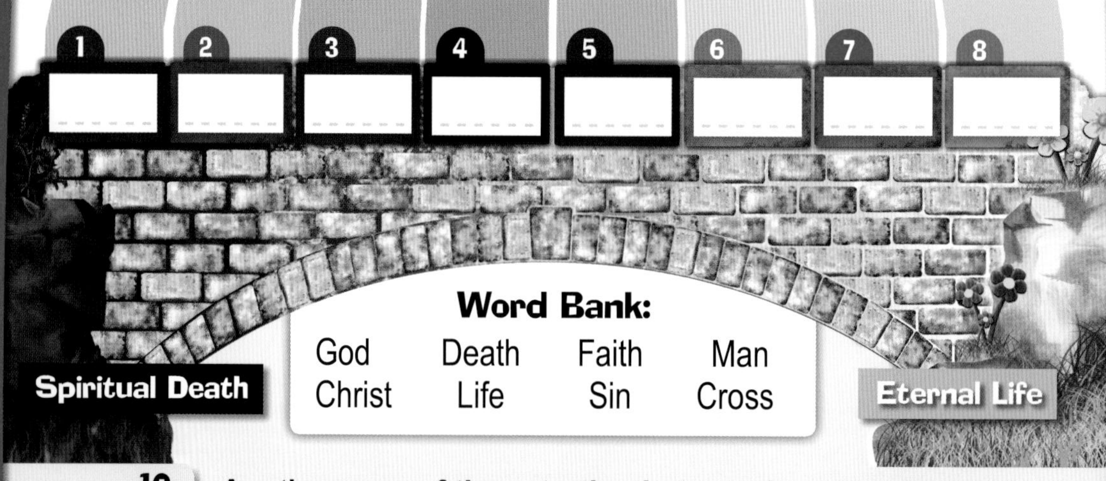

10. **Are there any of these truths that you do not understand clearly? If so, which ones?**

11. **Now, explain step-by-step the ChronoBridge to someone—parent, friend, teacher, or someone else. With whom will you share the ChronoBridge?**

Our Memory Verse:
John 5:24

Truly, truly, I say to you, whoever hears my word and believes him who sent me has eternal life. He does not come into judgment, but has passed from death to life.

Practice learning the verse by writing it below:

Reference:

Verse:

The Joy of Confidence:

Having Assurance of Our Salvation Gives Us Confidence

1. Since you accepted Jesus Christ as your Savior, have you ever wondered if you really were saved AT THAT TIME?

   ❍ YES

   ❍ NO

2. And if you are sure that you really were saved then, have you wondered if you are still saved NOW?

   ❍ YES

   ❍ NO

Doubts about your salvation can be good or they can be bad.

Doubts are **good**, if there is a REAL reason why you need to make sure you are saved.

Doubts are bad if Satan is using them to cause you to not trust God's promises.

The Bible can help you know for sure that you ARE saved. And the Bible can help you to know that your salvation is secure forever and ever.

3

How Can You Know You ARE REALLY Saved?

Find the Meaning: Witness

A witness can be something that proves that what has happened is true. Or it can be a person who tells the truth about what has happened.

★ **God has given FOUR WITNESSES that help you know that you are really saved, if you trusted in Jesus to save you.**

Witness #1

1. God

Read John 5:24.

If you have really believed Jesus died for you, what does this verse say about you?

-
-
-

Witness #2

2. The Bible

Read 1 John 5:11-13.

- Do you have the Son (Jesus)?
  ▢ YES ▢ NO
- Then, do you have eternal life?
  ▢ YES ▢ NO

Witness #3

3. Inner Witness

Read Romans 8:16.

Who lets you know in your spirit that you are God's child?

Witness #4

4. Changed Life

Read 2 Corinthians 5:17.

Have you had a change in your behavior since you were saved?

How Can You Know You WILL STAY Saved?

You are secure in the hands of Jesus and God the Father.

Underline all the words in **John 10:27-30** that promise you are secure because you have believed.

"My sheep hear My voice, and I know them, and they follow Me. And I give them eternal life, and they shall never perish; neither shall anyone snatch them out of My hand. My Father, who has given them to Me, is greater than all; and no one is able to snatch them out of My Father's hand. I and My Father are one."

You are safe and secure from all who accuse you.

5. Who or what can separate us from God's love? Read Romans 8:31-39.

You are sealed by the Holy Spirit of God.

When Jesus was on earth, important documents were rolled up and sealed with a dot of wax so no one would break the seal. When we believe in Jesus as our Savior, the Holy Spirit is the seal that protects us from becoming unsecured.

6. How long does this seal last? Read Ephesians 1:13-14.

3

Feelings: Can You Trust Them?

Christians can be tricked by their feelings. Sometimes you might think that you are not saved because you think, "I just don't *feel* saved." There are **three** words you need to know to help you when your feelings are different from what the Bible says.

Facts: What God has promised about salvation in the Bible is true. These wonderful promises are facts that will never change. You must trust the facts in the Bible.

Faith: The strength of your faith may change from one time to another, but that does not change the facts of God's promises. If you simply trust the facts of what God has promised, your faith will become strong again.

Feelings: Your feelings may change even more than your faith. But this doesn't change the facts in the Bible. Trust the Bible facts and your feelings will not jump around.

7. Can you explain this illustration in your own words?

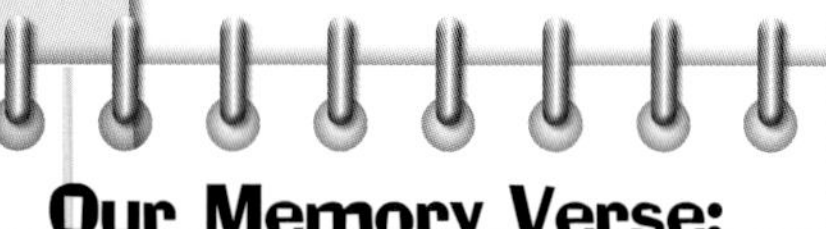

Our Memory Verse:
John 10:28

I give them eternal life, and they will never perish, and no one will snatch them out of my hand.

Practice learning the verse by writing it below:

Reference:

Verse:

The Joy of Guidance: 4

Reading God's Word Gives Us Guidance

What do you think about the Bible?

Put a check mark beside any of the following statements that express what **you** think about the Bible:

- ❑ It's a very LARGE book!
- ❑ The Bible seems boring to me.
- ❑ It's a difficult book to understand.
- ❑ I think the Bible is a special book, but I'm not sure why.
- ❑ I have never read any of the Bible.
- ❑ I don't see how the Bible relates to my life.
- ❑ I think the Bible would help me if I read it often and carefully.
- ❑ I don't have a Bible of my own.
- ❑ I have a Bible but think I need a different one.
- ❑ I would like to read and study the Bible, but I'm not sure how to do that.

Be prepared to discuss these statements with your discipleship leader.

This lesson will help you understand why the Bible is a special book and why you should read it. You will also learn some very simple but important tips about how to read the Bible so you can understand it and so it will give you guidance from God.

4

The Bible is a Book Inspired by God for an Important Purpose

Find the Meaning: Inspired

In the Bible, "inspired" means God guided the men who wrote the Bible so they wrote what God wanted to be in the Bible. The Bible contains true stories and important truths God wants everyone to know.

1. What do these verses say about how the Bible was written? Read 2 Peter 1:20-21.

2 Peter 1:20-21

Knowing this first, that no prophecy of Scripture is of any private interpretation, for prophecy never came by the will of man, but holy men of God spoke as they were moved by the Holy Spirit.

2 Timothy 3:16-17

All Scripture is given by inspiration of God, and is profitable for doctrine, for reproof, for correction, for instruction in righteousness, that the man of God may be complete, thoroughly equipped for every good work.

2. How was the Bible given to us? Read 2 Timothy 3:16-17.

3. What are four things 2 Timothy 3:16-17 tells us the Bible is useful ("profitable") for?

-
-
-
-

4. If a person reads, learns, and obeys the Bible, what will he become? Read 2 Timothy 3:17.

Because the Bible is inspired by God, you should...

Desire God's Word
Read 1 Peter 2:2.

5. Why should you desire (or long for) the Bible?

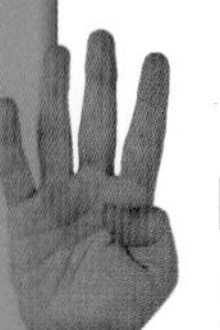

Study God's Word
Read 2 Timothy 2:15.

6. Why should you study the Bible?

Memorize God's Word
Psalm 119:11.

7. Why should you memorize the Bible?

Love God's Word
Read Psalm 119:97.

8. If you love the Bible, what will you do throughout the day? *Meditation means "to think about."*

When you desire the Bible, study it, memorize it, and love it, the Bible will guide you.

Psalm 119:105

Your word is a lamp to my feet and a light to my path.

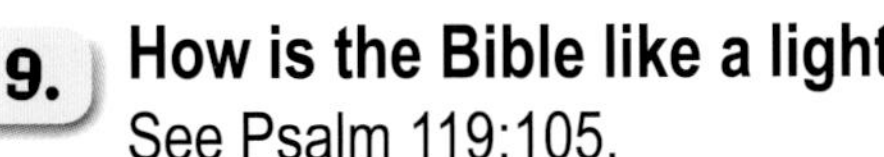

Think:

If you were walking on a dark and rocky path, how would a bright light help you?

9. **How is the Bible like a light?**
See Psalm 119:105.

4

Practical Tips for Reading and Studying the Bible

- **Pray before you read.** Ask God to help you understand the Bible. (See Psalm 119:18.)
- **Use a Bible reading plan** so you can read a little bit of the Bible regularly. You may want to read a chapter a day from a book of the Bible, like you are doing now with the devotional plan on pages 54-64.
- **Underline or circle Bible verses** or words that are special to you or that you think are especially important. You may want to write notes in a notebook about what you read, like you are doing with the devotional plan in this study.
- As you read, **ask God to help you understand** anything you do not understand. You can also ask your discipleship leader or someone else who can explain what you have read.
- **End your Bible reading with prayer.** Thank God for what He helped you learn. Ask Him to help you obey what you learned.
- **Tell other Christians** what you learned in your Bible reading.

Read the verses below that make important statements about God's Word and how we should respond. Practice underlining or putting a circle around the word or words that are special to you.

Joshua 1:8

This Book of the Law shall not depart from your mouth, but you shall meditate on it day and night, so that you may be careful to do according to all that is written in it. For then you will make your way prosperous, and then you will have good success.

Psalm 119:72, 89, 105

72 The law of your mouth is better to me than thousands of gold and silver pieces.

89 Forever, O Lord, your word is firmly fixed in the heavens.

105 Your word is a lamp to my feet and a light to my path.

Our Memory Verses: 1 Peter 2:2-3

Like newborn infants, long for the pure spiritual milk, that by it you may grow up into salvation—if indeed you have tasted that the Lord is good.

Practice learning the verses by writing them below:

Reference:

Verses:

The Joy of Prayer: 5

Talking with God Brings Us Closer to Him

1. Why do you think it is important for you to pray to God?

2. Do you think it is important to God that you pray to Him?

What Is Prayer?

Prayer is more than asking God to do things for you or to give you things. Prayer should be a time when you talk to God like you would your best friend. You know He is listening, and you feel comfortable talking with Him.

What can you talk about?

- Your sins
- How awesome He is
- The good things He does for you
- What you need
- What others need

We Pray...

- **To God the Father.** Read Matthew 6:9.
- **Through Jesus Christ.** Read Hebrews 4:14-16.
- **With the help of the Holy Spirit.** Read Romans 8:26.

3. **Which of the Bible passages do you need help to understand?**

Four Kinds of Prayer

- **C-**onfession
- **A-**doration and Praise
- **T-**hanksgiving
- **S-**upplication and Intercession

An easy way to remember the four kinds of prayer is to read the first letter on each line. ***They spell CATS.***

Confession

"Confession" is you agreeing with God about what you have done wrong.

4. **Why is it important to confess your sins at the beginning of your prayer?** Read Psalm 66:18.

C

Adoration and Praise

"Adoration" is when you feel great love for someone. "I love God very much!" "Praise" is expressing adoration for the thoughts or feelings you have. "What a wonderful God we serve!"

5. **What are some phrases the psalmist David used to show he adored God?** Read Psalm 145:1-3, 8-9, 13, 17-20.

Thanksgiving

"Thanksgiving" is showing or telling God (or others) how thankful you are for what He has (or they have) done.

6. **Which words tell what God is like in these verses?**
Read Psalm 107:1, 8, 15, 21, 31.

7. **What are some things God has done for you for which you can thank Him?**

Supplication and Intercession

"Supplication" is asking humbly and earnestly (very sincerely). "Intercession" is supplication for other people.

8. **What did Paul say to do whenever you are anxious (worried)?**
Read Philippians 4:6.

Now It's Your Turn!

Write a prayer to God using one of the four kinds of prayer.

Dear God,

In Jesus' name, Amen.

5

Practical Tips for Having a Daily Prayer Time

- **Write a list of what you should pray for**—your own needs and the needs of other people you know. Plan to pray every day for some of the needs on your prayer list.
- **Find a quiet and private place** where you can be alone every day to talk with God.
- It is good to begin your daily prayer time by **reading your Bible first** as we learned about in Lesson Four. You can then think about what you read when you pray and talk to God about what He showed you in the Bible.
- The Bible does not tell us when or how long we should pray. And the Bible does not tell us what position we should be in when we pray. **You want your time with God to be special** and have meaning for you. Choose how you will pray: on your knees, sitting, or standing.
- Try to **keep other thoughts from your mind** so you keep your thoughts focused on God when you pray.
- **Follow the CATS pattern for prayer:** Confession, Adoration and Praise, Thanksgiving, Supplication and Intercession.

9. What will make it hard for you to have a regular daily prayer time?

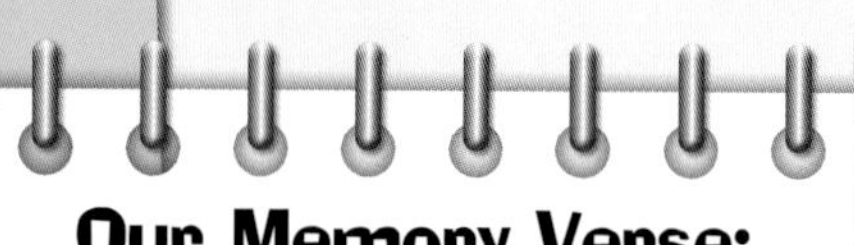

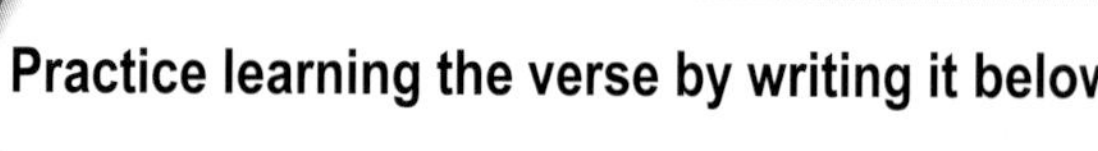

Our Memory Verse: Philippians 4:6

Do not be anxious about anything, but in everything by prayer and supplication with thanksgiving let your requests be made known to God.

Practice learning the verse by writing it below:

Reference:

Verse:

The Joy of God's Power: 6

The Holy Spirit in Us Gives Us Power to Live for God

1. Do you think it is sometimes hard to "do right" the way a Christian should?

2. Do you need help—especially God's help—to obey God? Or do you think you can do that without God's help?

There is only one true God. He exists in three persons as the Trinity: God the Father, God the Son (Jesus Christ), and God the Holy Spirit.

Father
is
is not
is not
God
is
is
Son
Holy Spirit
is not

People know more about God the Father and God the Son than they do about God the Holy Spirit.

The Holy Spirit is the power inside believers that helps them live as a Christian.

Some people do not understand what the Holy Spirit does.

The Holy Spirit does some important things for believers.

See if you can explain the above diagram to your discipleship leader.

6

The Holy Spirit: God Lives in Us

What Jesus Promised

Read John 14:16-17.

John 14:16-17

And I will ask the Father, and he will give you another Helper, to be with you forever, even the Spirit of truth, whom the world cannot receive, because it neither sees him nor knows him. You know him, for he dwells with you and will be in you.

3. What is another name for the Holy Spirit?

4. Who gives the Holy Spirit to believers?

5. How long does the Holy Spirit stay with believers?

6. What group of people cannot receive the Holy Spirit?

7. Where does the Holy Spirit live?

What Paul Knew Later

Read 1 Corinthians 6:19-20.

1 Corinthians 6:19-20

Or do you not know that your body is a temple of the Holy Spirit within you, whom you have from God? You are not your own, for you were bought with a price. So glorify God in your body.

8. What is your body called where the Holy Spirit lives?

9. What are believers to do?

In Corinth people did all kinds of wrong. Believers were tempted to live as they used to live before knowing Jesus. Paul wanted them to remember that the Holy Spirit lived in them, they should honor God, and not do wrong.

The Holy Spirit: God Helps Us

The word Jesus used in John 14:16 as a title for the Holy Spirit means "One called alongside" to be our Helper.

The Holy Spirit Helps Us Understand the Bible

Read 1 Corinthians 2:9-10, 12, 14.

God the Holy Spirit guided the men who wrote the Bible, so He can help you to understand what it says.

10. **How does God reveal (show) what He wants believers to know?**

The Holy Spirit Helps Us to Serve God

Read 1 Corinthians 12:1-11; Romans 12:6-8; and Ephesians 4:11, 12. *These passages list the spiritual gifts God gives believers.*

Spiritual gifts are special abilities that God gives believers so they can do His work. Some of the gifts that are still being given now are these:

- Teaching
- Showing mercy
- Encouraging others
- Serving or helping others
- Being a leader
- Giving to others

11. **Do you think God has given you any of these gifts and that the Holy Spirit is helping you to use them?**

☐ YES ☐ NO

12. **Which gift(s) do you think God has given you?**

6 The Holy Spirit: God Controls Us

The Holy Spirit Fills Our Life

Read Ephesians 5:18.

Ephesians 5:18
And do not be drunk with wine … but be filled with the Spirit.

Paul wrote this verse to the believers in the city of Ephesus.

13. **What were the believers to *stop* doing?**

14. **What were the believers to *start* doing?**

15. **Can you be controlled by bad behavior and by the Holy Spirit at the same time?** ▢ **YES** ▢ **NO**

The Holy Spirit Gives Us "Fruit"

Read Galatians 5:16-26.

A believer who allows the Holy Spirit to control him will:

- Live by the help of the Holy Spirit.
- Allow the Holy Spirit to lead him.
- Resist obeying the desire or the "want" to sin.
- Show the fruit of the Holy Spirit.

In your own words, define the fruit of the Spirit.

Love Joy
Peace
Patience
Kindness
Goodness
Faithfulness
Gentleness
Self-Control

Our Memory Verses:

1 Corinthians 6:19-20

Or do you not know that your body is a temple of the Holy Spirit within you, whom you have from God? You are not your own, for you were bought with a price. So glorify God in your body.

Practice learning the verses by writing them below:

Reference:

Verses:

The Joy of Purity: 7

Obeying God's Word Helps Us Live Pure Lives that Please Him

King David's Sin
Read 2 Samuel 11:14-27.

King David fell in love with another man's wife. He then ordered that man to go into battle, to a place where the man would surely be killed.

King David's Confession
Read Psalm 51:1-17.

These verses record David's prayer of confession—prayer for forgiveness and cleansing.

1. **How did David feel?**

2. **What did he want?**
See verses 1-2, 7-8, 9-10, 12.

"Create in me a clean heart, O God, and renew a right spirit within me."
Psalm 51:10

7

God's Standards: Holiness and Righteousness

3. How do you feel when you do something wrong?

4. Why do you feel that way?

God's standards (rules for living) for Himself and His people are:

- Holiness (means separation from sin)
- Righteousness (means doing what is right)

Holiness

Read 1 Peter 1:14-16.

5. What will "obedient" believers not do?

6. Why should believers want to be holy?

7. *True or False? Circle one.*

A believer who desires to live a holy life tries to separate him-self/herself from sin and wants to honor God everyday.

Righteousness

Read Psalm 15:1-2.

8. Verse one asks "Who can come into God's presence (be close to Him)?"

9. Verse two answers that question in three ways that mean the same thing:

-
-
-

Your Response: Obedience or Disobedience

Sin is disobeying the laws God gave to us in the Bible. Just as Satan tempted Adam and Eve in the Garden of Eden, he tempts us to disobey God.

Temptations to Be Resisted

Read 1 John 2:15-17. The "world" in these verses does not mean our universe. It means all that is against God and what He wants for His people.

10. **What are three kinds of temptations?**

-
-
-

11. **What happens if we "walk by the Spirit"?** Read Galatians 5:16-17.

Resisting Temptations

Read James 4:7.

12. **What can you do to make the devil flee from you?**

13. **In Matthew 4:1-11, what did Jesus do each time to resist the devil?**

Read Matthew 4:1-11 and then draw a line between the temptations that match.

	Jesus was tempted by:
"desires of the flesh"	*kingdoms of the world*
"desires of the eyes"	*jump off the temple, angels protect*
"pride of life"	*stones to bread*

Promised Help to Resist Temptations

Read 1 Corinthians 10:13.

Put a check mark beside each promise found in this verse.

- ❍ Your temptations are common to other people.
- ❍ God will always provide a way to escape temptations.
- ❍ God is faithful.
- ❍ God will not allow temptations beyond your ability to resist.

7

God's Mercy: Forgiveness and Cleansing

Find the Meaning: Confess

Confess means you agree with God about your sin. You admit that you have disobeyed God's standards (rules).

Read 1 John 1:9. (Memory verse at bottom of this page)

14. What do you need to do to receive God's mercy (kindness)?

15. What does God do?

Read Psalm 32:1-5. Think about the story of King David (page 35). David confessed his sin and God forgave him. This is what 1 John 1:9 says believers should do and what God will do.

16. If "blessed" means a special kind of happiness, how did David feel when his sin was forgiven? (vv. 1-2)

17. Before he confessed his sin, how did David feel? (vv. 3-4)

18. What should you do when you sin?

Our Memory Verse:
1 John 1:9

If we confess our sins, he is faithful and just to forgive us our sins and to cleanse us from all unrighteousness.

Practice learning the verse by writing it below:

Reference:

Verse:

The Joy of Sharing: 8

Telling Others about Jesus Is a Privilege God Has Given Us

The gospel is the "good news" that Jesus died on the cross and rose from the grave to pay our sin debt and give us eternal life. It is a privilege for us to share this good news with people who have not trusted Jesus to be their Savior. But, it is also an important responsibility that we should not neglect.

How Do You Feel?

Does it frighten you or make you nervous to tell other people how they can be saved—how they can have their sins forgiven and become Christ-followers? If so, what are the reasons for your fears?

- ☐ I am afraid that I will not know what to say.
- ☐ I am afraid that the person will be upset with me.
- ☐ I am afraid that the person will ask me a question that I cannot answer.
- ☐ There is another reason that I am afraid but it is not mentioned here.

This lesson will help you with some of these fears.

8

Share the Gospel by Using the ChronoBridge to Life

From memory, try to write the ***eight very important Bible truths*** in the proper places on the bridge. Do the best you can from memory, then turn to pages 14-17 if you need to see them.

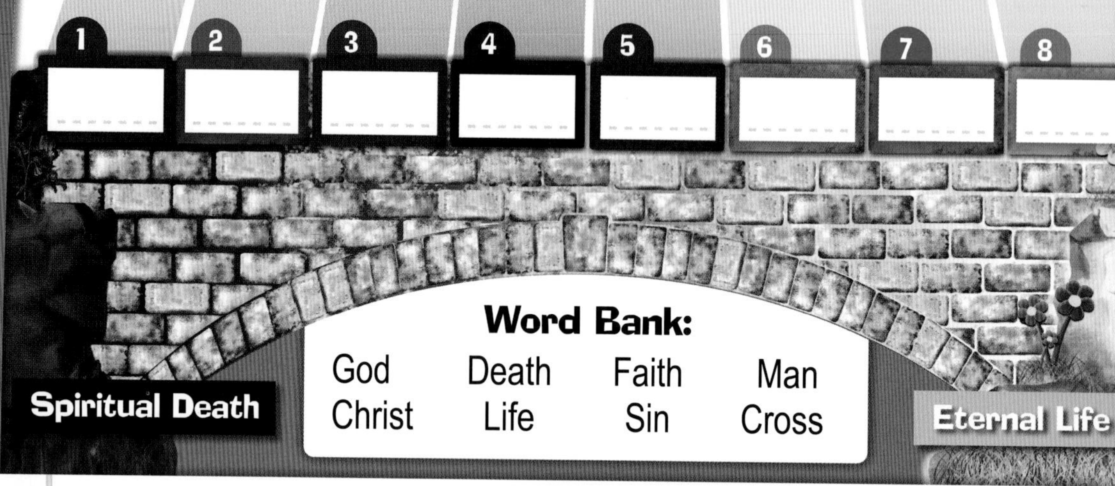

Practice Activity:

Use a piece of paper and a pen or pencil. Pretend that you want to share the gospel with a friend, using the Chronological Bridge to Life.

Suppose you only have a pen or pencil and a blank piece of paper. With your discipleship leader or another friend, practice sharing the gospel with him or her using the bridge.

1. Draw a simple bridge.

2. Add the eight words and explain each part of the gospel story as you add the words to the bridge.

3. Invite your practice partner to ask you questions after you finish.

Share the Gospel by Telling Your Own Story

We call this a "faith story"—a story about how you placed your faith in Jesus to be your Savior.
There are three parts of your faith story:

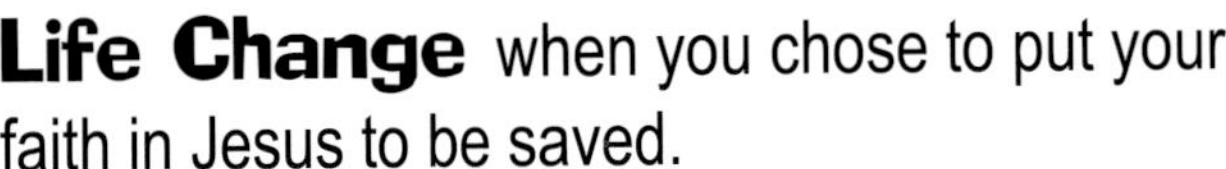

Life Before you put your faith in Jesus to be saved.

Tell what your life was like before you were saved, before you admitted to God that you were a sinner and needed to trust Jesus to forgive your sins and make you a child of God.

Life Change when you chose to put your faith in Jesus to be saved.

- *Tell your story of how you began to know that you were a sinner.*
- *Tell how you began to understand the gospel. Tell how you learned the gospel truths—who told you and what they said that helped you to understand the gospel story.*
- *Tell what happened to cause you to decide to trust Jesus as your Savior. Just tell it the way it happened.*

Life Now since you put your faith in Jesus to be saved.

Tell how your life has been different and better since the time you trusted Jesus to be your Savior.

With the help of your discipleship leader or a Christian parent or friend, think about each part of your faith story. Make some notes on each part. Work on it until you are comfortable sharing it.

You may need to work on and practice it several times before you can tell it clearly and easily.

8

How to Start Sharing the Gospel

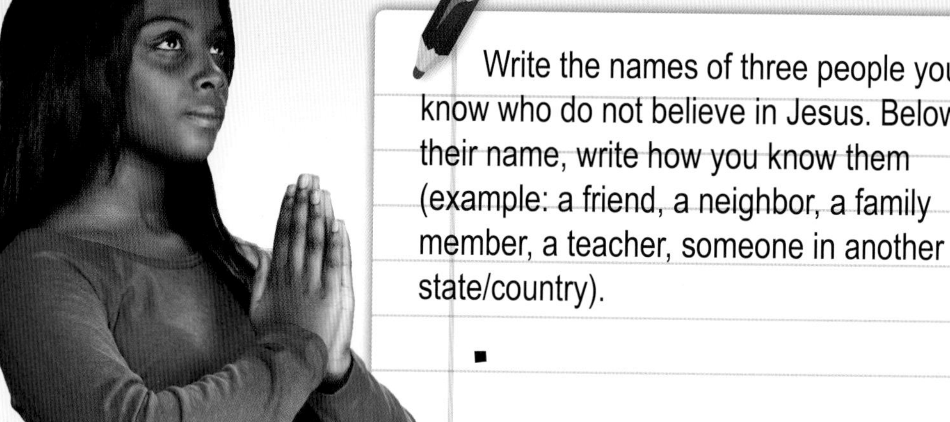

Write the names of three people you know who do not believe in Jesus. Below their name, write how you know them (example: a friend, a neighbor, a family member, a teacher, someone in another state/country).

-
-
-

Plan how you can witness (share the gospel) with one of these people.

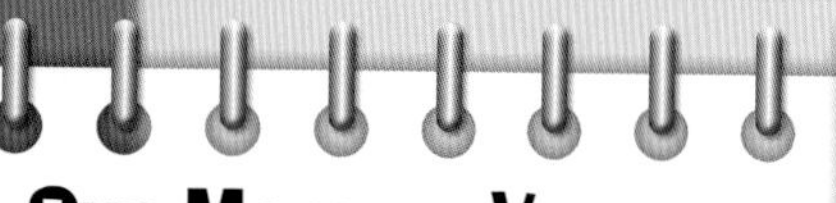

What is one way you could share the gospel with them?

Pray regularly for the people on your list that:

- they would want to know God.
- they would believe what the Bible says.
- God would use you or someone else to share the gospel with them.
- they would believe in Jesus as Savior.

Our Memory Verses: John 1:41-42a

He first found his own brother Simon and said to him, "We have found the Messiah" (which means Christ). He brought him to Jesus.

Practice learning the verses by writing them below:

Reference:

Verses:

The Joy of Fellowship:

A Bible-Believing Church Gives You a Sense of Belonging

▶ **There are so many churches! How will I know which churches are closest to the teachings of the Bible?**

Read the following description of things you should look for to know if a church is good, according to what the Bible teaches. **Underline specific things you should look for in a church.** Then, discuss these with your discipleship leader.

Description of What a Good Bible-Believing Church Is and Does

▶ The Bible teaches that Christians are to **meet together as a group of believers** called a "church." Individual churches are called "local churches." A local church should believe and teach that the **Bible is God's inspired Word**, from beginning to end.

▶ These **believers are to be baptized** and they are to meet to **fellowship and pray together** regularly. Their leaders are one or more "pastors" and "deacons." Sometimes the leaders are called "elders."

▶ As a church, the **believers practice baptism and the Lord's Supper**. These are called ordinances (an order from God). Believers **study the Bible**, **worship** and **serve** God together. They **evangelize** (tell others the gospel) and make disciples (help new believers know the Bible and follow God).

▶ When believers in the church reach out to unbelievers and help them believe in Jesus, this can lead to **starting new churches** in their own country and to **sending missionaries** to other parts of the world.

Baptism for Believers

What Baptism Means

Read Romans 6:4.

Romans 6:4

We were buried therefore with him by baptism into death, in order that, just as Christ was raised from the dead by the glory of the Father, we too might walk in newness of life.

Find the three phrases in Romans 6:4 that are shown in the drawings below. Write each phrase below the correct drawing.

1

2

3

What Is Required for Baptism

Read Acts 16:30-33.

1. What must a person do before being baptized?

2. Which one of these do you think is true?

- ▢ A person must be baptized in order to be saved.
- ▢ Baptism does not save a person, it only shows what Jesus did for us by dying on the cross and being raised from the dead. It demonstrates that a person wants the world to know that he or she is now a true believer, a Christ-follower.

The Lord's Supper

The Purposes of the Lord's Supper Read 1 Corinthians 11:23-26.

For true believers—*people who have trusted Jesus as Savior:*

3. The Lord's Supper helps believers to remember Christ's death. Why is it important to remember Christ's death regularly? (vs. 26, 28)

For unbelievers—*people who have not trusted Jesus as Savior:*

The Lord's Supper helps unbelievers to *see* and *hear* Christ's death talked about. They see the bread and communion juice which are symbols of Christ's death. They hear the pastor explain the meaning of the Lord's Supper and how only believers can participate.

The Lord's Supper Unites Believers

Read 1 Corinthians 10:17.

The Lord's Supper is sometimes called "communion." This word means fellowship or unity. When believers meet and eat the Lord's Supper, they are coming together to remember why Christ died.

What about You?

4. What do you not understand about baptism or the Lord's Supper?

5. Have you been baptized since you trusted Jesus Christ as your personal Savior? If no, what is keeping you from this step of obedience to Jesus?

9

The Ministry of a Local Church

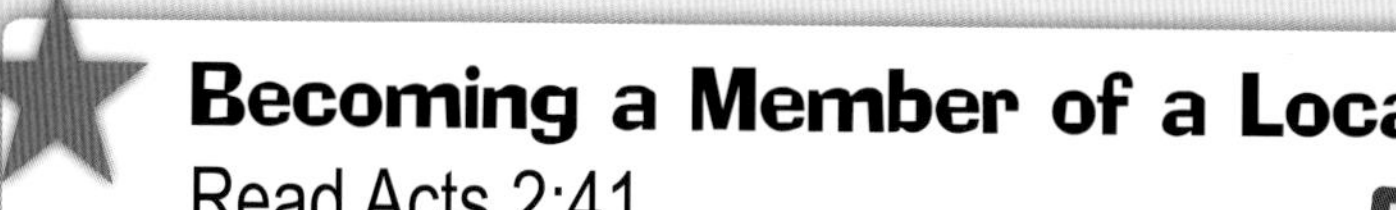

Becoming a Member of a Local Church

Read Acts 2:41.

6. On the day that is mentioned in this verse, 3,000 people were added to the church! **What two things did they do in order to be qualified to be a member of the church?**

- **First:**
- **Second:**

Acts 2:41

So those who received his word were baptized, and there were added that day about three thousand souls.

Meeting Together in the Local Church

Read Hebrews 10:24-25.

7. **Why does God want us to go to church regularly?**

Purposes of a Bible-Teaching Local Church

The church uses the Bible and:

- teaches you how to worship God. *John 4:23-24* **Worship**
- trains you to help others. *Ephesians 4:11-12* **Service**
- sends you to reach unsaved people. *Mark 16:15* **Evangelism**

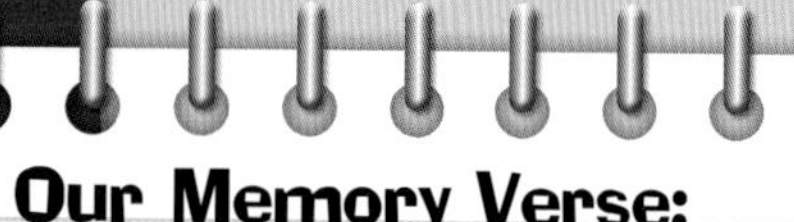

Our Memory Verse:
Hebrews 10:25

Not neglecting to meet together, as is the habit of some, but encouraging one another, and all the more as you see the Day drawing near.

Practice learning the verse by writing it below:

Reference:

Verse:

The Joy of Service: 10

Understanding God's Plan for You Gives You a Sense of Purpose

1. Why doesn't God take us immediately to Heaven when we are saved? Choose the best answer.

- ❍ Because He does not want to separate us from our family and friends on Earth.
- ❍ Because Heaven is not yet ready for us.
- ❍ Because He has a purpose for us to accomplish here on Earth.

Just before Jesus left Earth to go back to Heaven, He gave to His followers what we call the "Great Commission."

Matthew 28:19-20

"Go therefore and make disciples of all nations, baptizing them in the name of the Father and of the Son and of the Holy Spirit, teaching them to observe all that I have commanded you. And behold, I am with you always, to the end of the age."

2. The Great Commission gives every Christ-follower several purposes for living. **What are the purposes you see in Matthew 28:19-20?**

God has given you a purpose in...

Evangelism

3. Do you know what "evangelism" is? See if you can define it in your own words. Hint: Lesson 8 was about evangelism, even though we did not use that word there.

4. Have you been able to explain the *Chronological Bridge to Life* to someone since you learned it?

- ☐ **YES** If you have, what happened?
- ☐ **NO** If you have not, think of someone you could explain the ChronoBridge to and when you might be able to do that.

Ministry in Your Church

Lesson 9 was about serving ("ministering") in your local church.

5. Have you been attending your church regularly?

☐ **YES** ☐ **NO**

6. What are some things that you could do to be a helper in your church?

7. If you cannot think of something you can do, whom could you ask? Circle one of these.

Your Pastor	**Your Parent**	**Your Teacher**	**Other:** Who?

Discipleship

What is discipleship?

Discipleship is when a believer, who loves and obeys God, helps a believer who is just learning to love and obey God and the Bible. The mature believer helps the less mature believer:

- to understand what he believes,
- to learn how to read the Bible and pray regularly,
- to become more like Christ in how he acts, and
- to share the gospel and disciple others who need it.

8. **Who needs to be discipled?**

9. **Who can be a disciple maker?**

10. **Can you think of someone that you could disciple—that you could come alongside and help become a more mature Christian?**

Look at the pictures.

11. **Do they give you an idea of what you might do to disciple one of your Christian friends? What would that be?**

As you get older, God may want to use you for two other purposes:

Help Start a New Church

12. Is there a place in the area where you live that needs a church that teaches the Bible and preaches the gospel? Ask your discipleship leader where a place might be. Begin praying that God would send someone there to start a good local church.

Become a Missionary

13. What can I do *now* to begin learning what it would be like to be a missionary?

- Start reading missionary biographies
- Talk to missionaries who visit your church
- Go on a short-term missions trip when you are a teenager
- Study to find parts of the world that need missionaries
- Ask God if He might want you to become a missionary

Are you willing to ask God if He wants you to be an overseas missionary someday, so you can make disciples in another country?

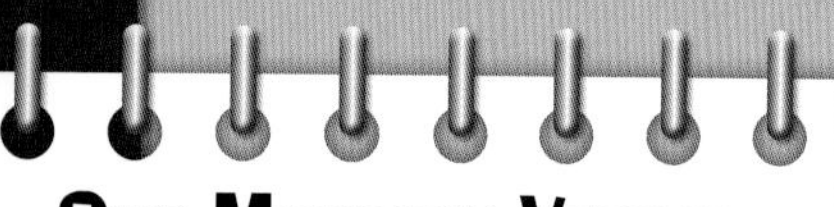

Our Memory Verse:
Ephesians 2:10

For we are his workmanship, created in Christ Jesus for good works, which God prepared beforehand, that we should walk in them.

Practice learning the verse by writing it below:

Reference:

Verse:

Review Activity Instructions

Let's see what you remember about The Way to Joy from the ten lessons in this book! Pages 51 to 53 have one fun—and different—review activity for each lesson. Follow the directions for each activity. If you can't remember an answer, turn to the lesson for that activity in this booklet, re-read the lesson, then come back to the activity and write the answer.

1 The Joy of Hope

Use the numbers to complete the sentences.

Important Numbers to Know

1
2
40
66
1,500

- The Bible is _______ Book.
- There are ________ books in the Bible.
- The Bible was written by _______ authors who lived at different times.
- It took _________ years to write the Bible.
- The stories in the Bible make ______ BIG Story.
- Part _____ is the Old Testament.
- Part _____ is the New Testament.

2 The Joy of Eternal Life

Draw a line to match the ChronoBridge word with the description.

God	Promised to those who put their trust in Jesus.
Man	Sinless Son of God and only way to eternal life.
Sin	Faith is the gift of God, not a result of works.
Death	Creator and Judge.
Christ	Made by God.
Cross	Man will die and be judged by God.
Faith	All have sinned and deserve punishment.
Life	Jesus bore our sins in his body on the tree.

3 The Joy of Confidence

From memory, write the answers in the spaces indicated.

What are the Four Witnesses that help you know you are saved?

1.
2.
3.
4.

Who or what can separate you from God's love?

What are three words to remember when your feelings are different from what the Bible says?

F

F

F

4 The Joy of Guidance

Unscramble the words and write them in the spaces.

Because the Bible is God's inspired book (Word), you should:

Deeris: ______________________ it.

Dystu: ______________________ it.

Zemomeri: ______________________ it.

Velo: ______________________ it.

When you do this, the Bible will guide you.

5 The Joy of Prayer

Write the four kinds of prayer, using the acrostic below.

C-

A-

T-

S-

6 The Joy of God's Power

Fill in the missing words in the diagram to explain the Trinity. There are 9 blanks.

7 The Joy of Purity

Obeying God's Word helps you to live a pure life that pleases Him.

▶ What Bible verse tells you what to do when you sin?

Print the verse and reference in the space provided.

8 The Joy of Sharing: *ChronoBridge*

Write one sentence that you would use to explain each of the Eight Very Important Truths with someone who does not know God.

God

Man

Sin

Death

Christ

Cross

Faith

Life

9 The Joy of Fellowship

Draw stick figure drawings to illustrate each of the 3 parts of Baptism.

Baptism

1

2

3

Draw the parts of the Lord's Supper.

The Lord's Supper

10 The Joy of Service

To learn three purposes God has for you, answer the questions and ask God to give you opportunities to share, serve, and help.

1. Evangelize: Who will you share the *ChronoBridge to Life* with and when?

2. Serve in Your Church: What is one way you can help in church?

3. Disciple: Who could you help to love and obey God and the Bible better? (Maybe you could use *The Way to Joy—Kids* with that person.)

Instructions
for Using My Bible Reading Plan and Prayer Journal

You should pray and read your Bible every day, but for the next ten weeks, the pages in this Bible Reading Plan and Prayer Journal will give Bible references for just five days of each week. All of the chapters in the Bible Reading Plan are from the Old Testament book of Genesis, the first book in the Bible. Sometimes you will read an entire chapter, sometimes part of a chapter. Genesis is full of exciting stories that tell what happened in the beginning of the world and to the descendants of Adam and Eve.

1. Read the chapter assigned for the day and write down two responses:

- **One thing you learned from your reading.** Look especially for things that are most interesting or helpful to you.
- **One question that you have from your Bible reading.** You may want to ask your discipleship leader or someone else to help you learn the answer to this question.

2. Review and practice the Bible memory verses that have been assigned to you in this discipleship study.

Work especially on the most recent verse assigned. But review all of them. Put a check mark in the box in front of "I Practiced My Memory Verses!" to show that you reviewed or practiced saying the memory verses.

3. Choose one special prayer focus for the day and write it down before you pray. Then have your personal prayer time.

Keep the CATS pattern in mind from Lesson 5. You do not have to always follow this specific pattern, but it is important to remember all elements of prayer and practice them when most appropriate.

Take a Look at This Example

Sample

Read:
Psalm 23

What is one thing I **LEARNED**?
God takes care of me like a shepherd takes care of sheep, and I should trust God always.

What is one **QUESTION** I have?
How can a rod and a staff provide comfort?

Today's Prayer Focus: My unsaved friends

I Practiced My **Memory Verses**!

My Bible Reading Plan and Prayer Journal

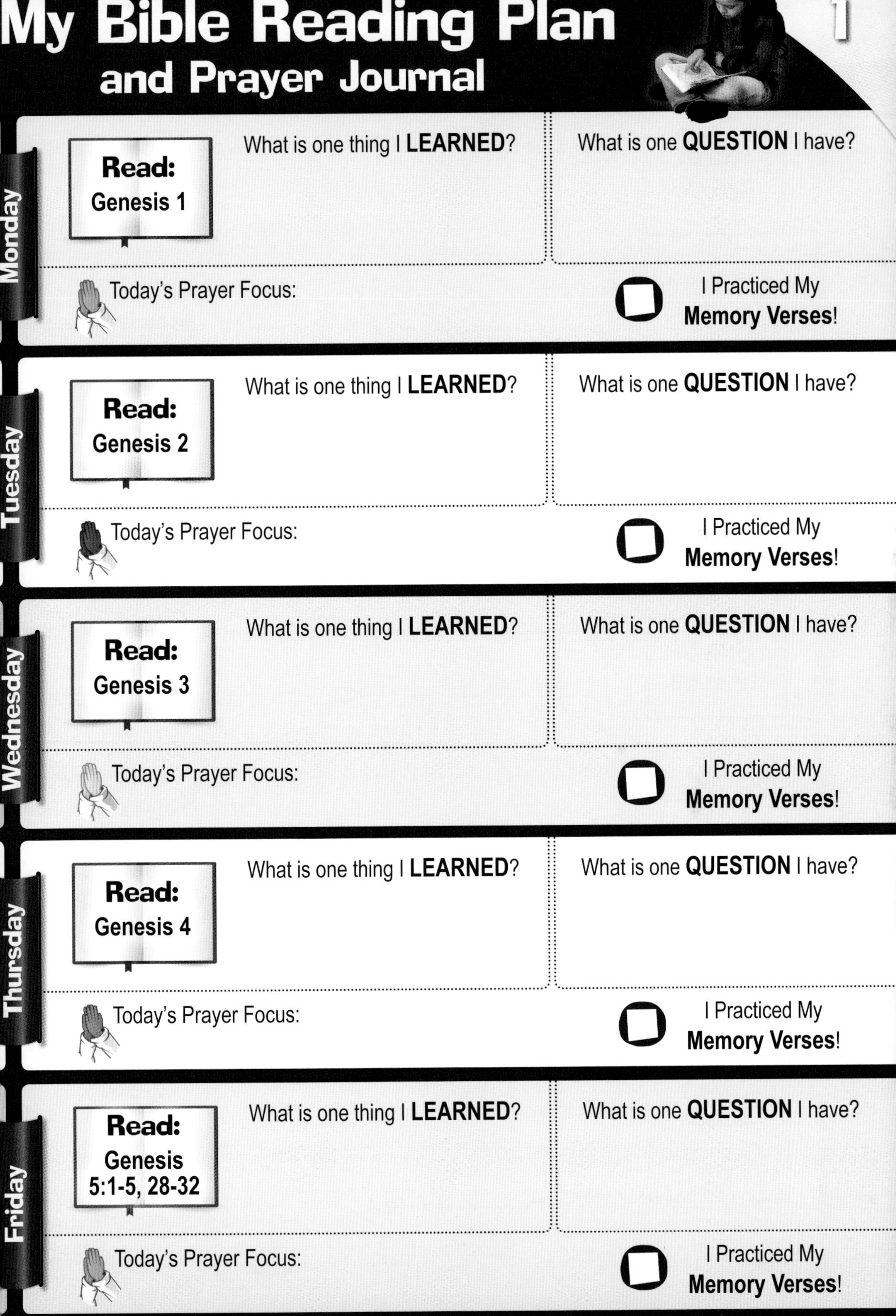

Monday

Read: Genesis 1

What is one thing I **LEARNED**?

What is one **QUESTION** I have?

Today's Prayer Focus:

☐ I Practiced My **Memory Verses**!

Tuesday

Read: Genesis 2

What is one thing I **LEARNED**?

What is one **QUESTION** I have?

Today's Prayer Focus:

☐ I Practiced My **Memory Verses**!

Wednesday

Read: Genesis 3

What is one thing I **LEARNED**?

What is one **QUESTION** I have?

Today's Prayer Focus:

☐ I Practiced My **Memory Verses**!

Thursday

Read: Genesis 4

What is one thing I **LEARNED**?

What is one **QUESTION** I have?

Today's Prayer Focus:

☐ I Practiced My **Memory Verses**!

Friday

Read: Genesis 5:1-5, 28-32

What is one thing I **LEARNED**?

What is one **QUESTION** I have?

Today's Prayer Focus:

☐ I Practiced My **Memory Verses**!

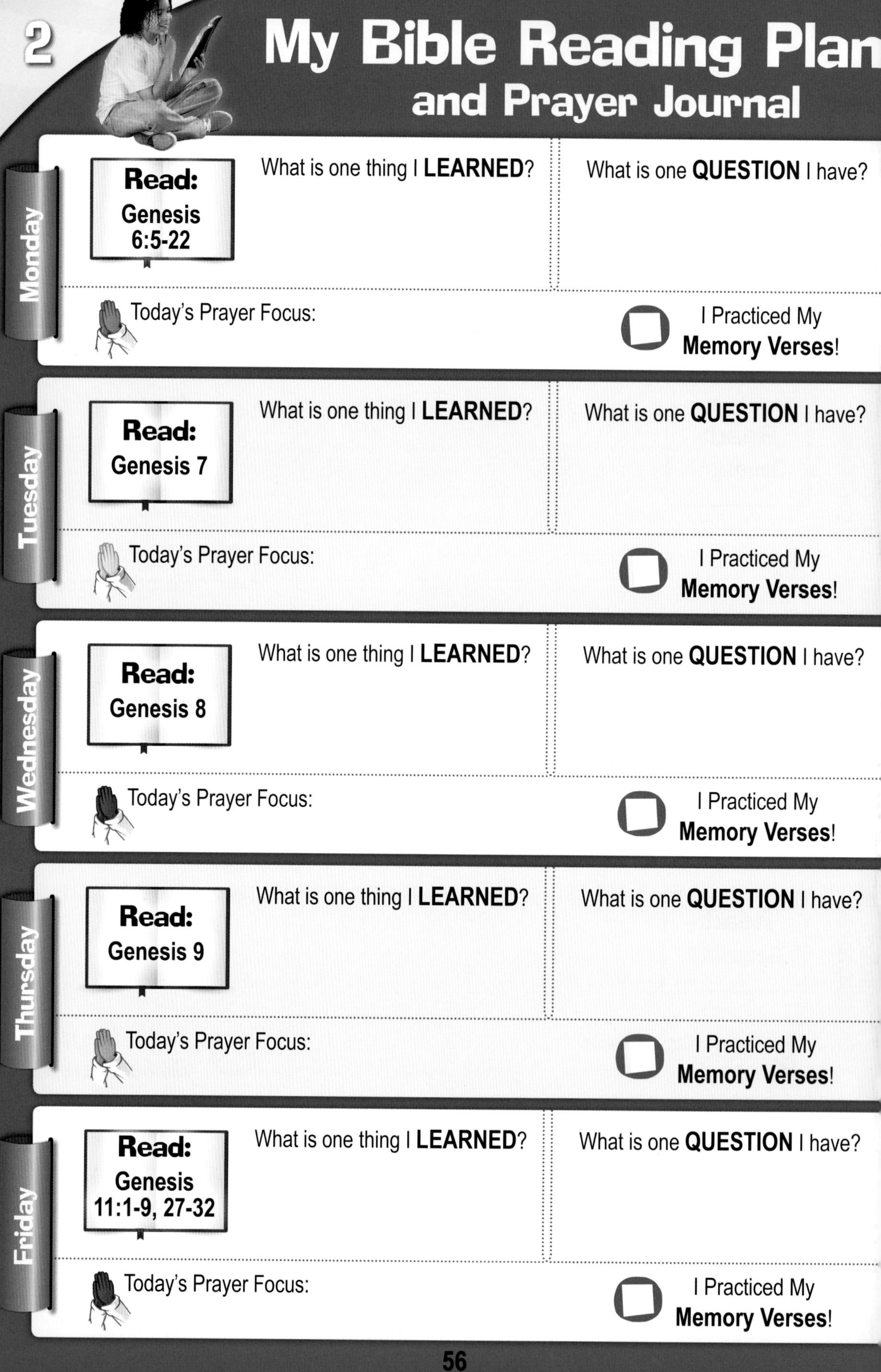

2

My Bible Reading Plan
and Prayer Journal

Monday

Read: Genesis 6:5-22

What is one thing I **LEARNED**?

What is one **QUESTION** I have?

Today's Prayer Focus:

I Practiced My **Memory Verses**!

Tuesday

Read: Genesis 7

What is one thing I **LEARNED**?

What is one **QUESTION** I have?

Today's Prayer Focus:

I Practiced My **Memory Verses**!

Wednesday

Read: Genesis 8

What is one thing I **LEARNED**?

What is one **QUESTION** I have?

Today's Prayer Focus:

I Practiced My **Memory Verses**!

Thursday

Read: Genesis 9

What is one thing I **LEARNED**?

What is one **QUESTION** I have?

Today's Prayer Focus:

I Practiced My **Memory Verses**!

Friday

Read: Genesis 11:1-9, 27-32

What is one thing I **LEARNED**?

What is one **QUESTION** I have?

Today's Prayer Focus:

I Practiced My **Memory Verses**!

My Bible Reading Plan
and Prayer Journal

3

Monday

Read: Genesis 12

What is one thing I **LEARNED**?

What is one QUESTION I have?

Today's Prayer Focus:

I Practiced My **Memory Verses**!

Tuesday

Read: Genesis 13

What is one thing I **LEARNED**?

What is one **QUESTION** I have?

Today's Prayer Focus:

I Practiced My **Memory Verses**!

Wednesday

Read: Genesis 14

What is one thing I **LEARNED**?

What is one **QUESTION** I have?

Today's Prayer Focus:

I Practiced My **Memory Verses**!

Thursday

Read: Genesis 15

What is one thing I **LEARNED**?

What is one **QUESTION** I have?

Today's Prayer Focus:

I Practiced My **Memory Verses**!

Friday

Read: Genesis 16

What is one thing I **LEARNED**?

What is one **QUESTION** I have?

Today's Prayer Focus:

I Practiced My **Memory Verses**!

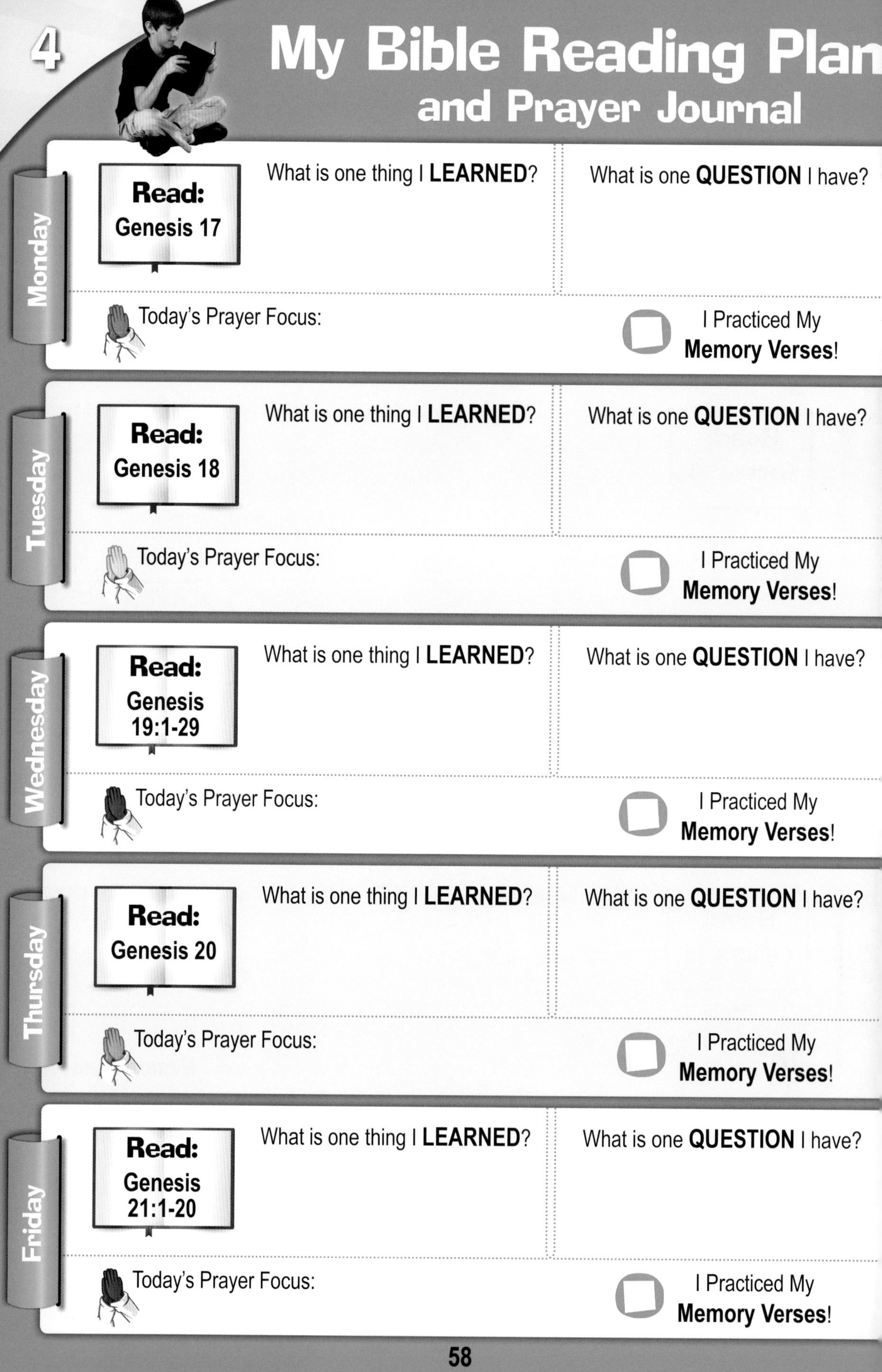

4

My Bible Reading Plan
and Prayer Journal

Monday

Read: Genesis 17

What is one thing I **LEARNED**?

What is one **QUESTION** I have?

Today's Prayer Focus:

I Practiced My **Memory Verses**!

Tuesday

Read: Genesis 18

What is one thing I **LEARNED**?

What is one **QUESTION** I have?

Today's Prayer Focus:

I Practiced My **Memory Verses**!

Wednesday

Read: Genesis 19:1-29

What is one thing I **LEARNED**?

What is one **QUESTION** I have?

Today's Prayer Focus:

I Practiced My **Memory Verses**!

Thursday

Read: Genesis 20

What is one thing I **LEARNED**?

What is one **QUESTION** I have?

Today's Prayer Focus:

I Practiced My **Memory Verses**!

Friday

Read: Genesis 21:1-20

What is one thing I **LEARNED**?

What is one **QUESTION** I have?

Today's Prayer Focus:

I Practiced My **Memory Verses**!

My Bible Reading Plan and Prayer Journal

5

Monday

Read: Genesis 22:1-19

What is one thing I **LEARNED**?

What is one **QUESTION** I have?

Today's Prayer Focus:

I Practiced My **Memory Verses**!

Tuesday

Read: Genesis 23

What is one thing I **LEARNED**?

What is one **QUESTION** I have?

Today's Prayer Focus:

I Practiced My **Memory Verses**!

Wednesday

Read: Genesis 24:1-28

What is one thing I **LEARNED**?

What is one **QUESTION** I have?

Today's Prayer Focus:

I Practiced My **Memory Verses**!

Thursday

Read: Genesis 24:29-62

What is one thing I **LEARNED**?

What is one **QUESTION** I have?

Today's Prayer Focus:

I Practiced My **Memory Verses**!

Friday

Read: Genesis 25:7-11, 19-34

What is one thing I **LEARNED**?

What is one **QUESTION** I have?

Today's Prayer Focus:

I Practiced My **Memory Verses**!

6

My Bible Reading Plan
and Prayer Journal

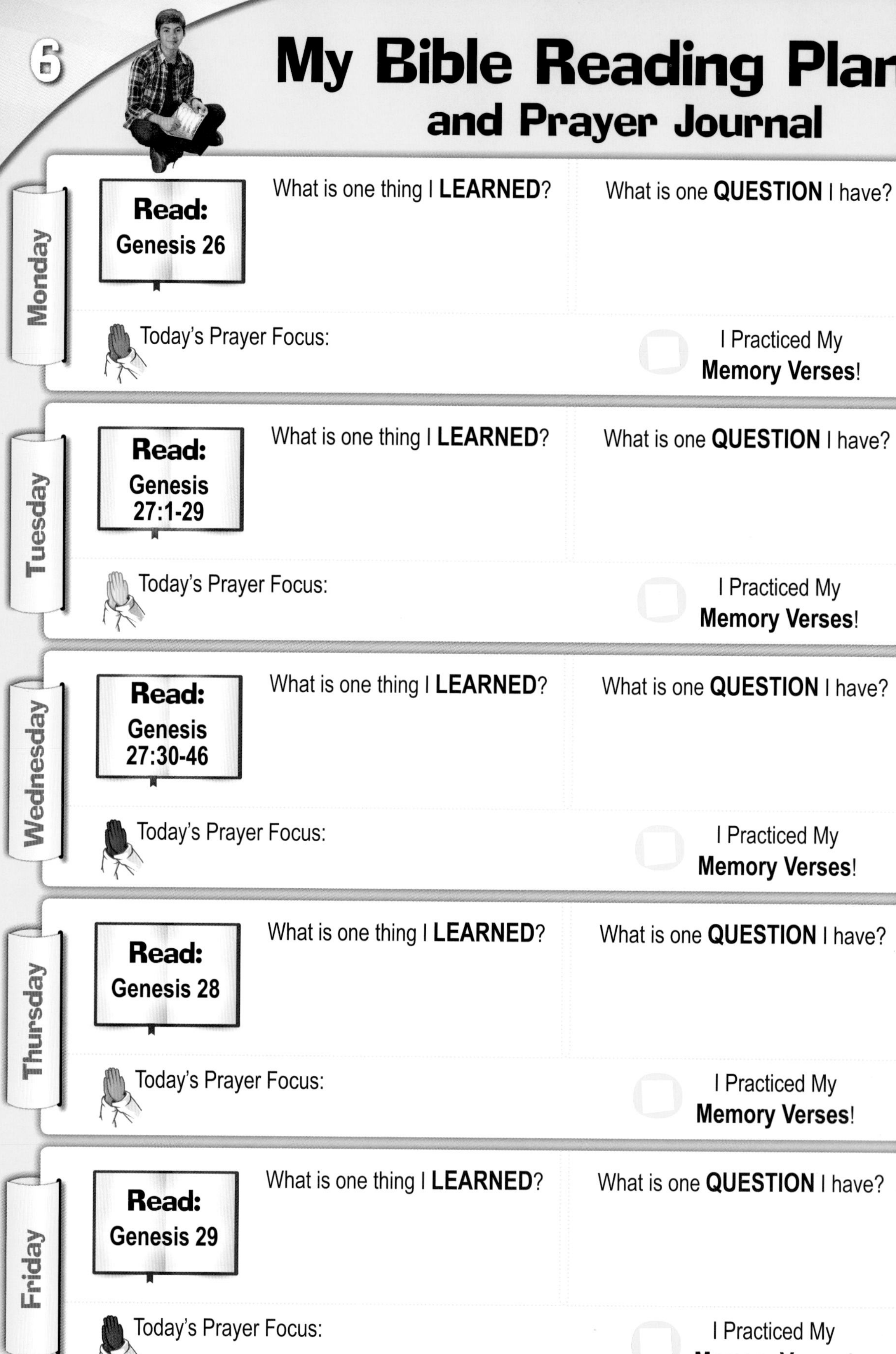

Monday

Read: Genesis 26

What is one thing I **LEARNED**?

What is one **QUESTION** I have?

Today's Prayer Focus:

I Practiced My **Memory Verses**!

Tuesday

Read: Genesis 27:1-29

What is one thing I **LEARNED**?

What is one **QUESTION** I have?

Today's Prayer Focus:

I Practiced My **Memory Verses**!

Wednesday

Read: Genesis 27:30-46

What is one thing I **LEARNED**?

What is one **QUESTION** I have?

Today's Prayer Focus:

I Practiced My **Memory Verses**!

Thursday

Read: Genesis 28

What is one thing I **LEARNED**?

What is one **QUESTION** I have?

Today's Prayer Focus:

I Practiced My **Memory Verses**!

Friday

Read: Genesis 29

What is one thing I **LEARNED**?

What is one **QUESTION** I have?

Today's Prayer Focus:

I Practiced My **Memory Verses**!

My Bible Reading Plan
and Prayer Journal

7

Monday

Read:
Genesis 30:1-21

What is one thing I **LEARNED**?

What is one **QUESTION** I have?

Today's Prayer Focus:

I Practiced My **Memory Verses**!

Tuesday

Read:
Genesis 30:22-43

What is one thing I **LEARNED**?

What is one **QUESTION** I have?

Today's Prayer Focus:

I Practiced My **Memory Verses**!

Wednesday

Read:
Genesis 31

What is one thing I **LEARNED**?

What is one **QUESTION** I have?

Today's Prayer Focus:

I Practiced My **Memory Verses**!

Thursday

Read:
Genesis 32

What is one thing I **LEARNED**?

What is one **QUESTION** I have?

Today's Prayer Focus:

I Practiced My **Memory Verses**!

Friday

Read:
Genesis 33

What is one thing I **LEARNED**?

What is one **QUESTION** I have?

Today's Prayer Focus:

I Practiced My **Memory Verses**!

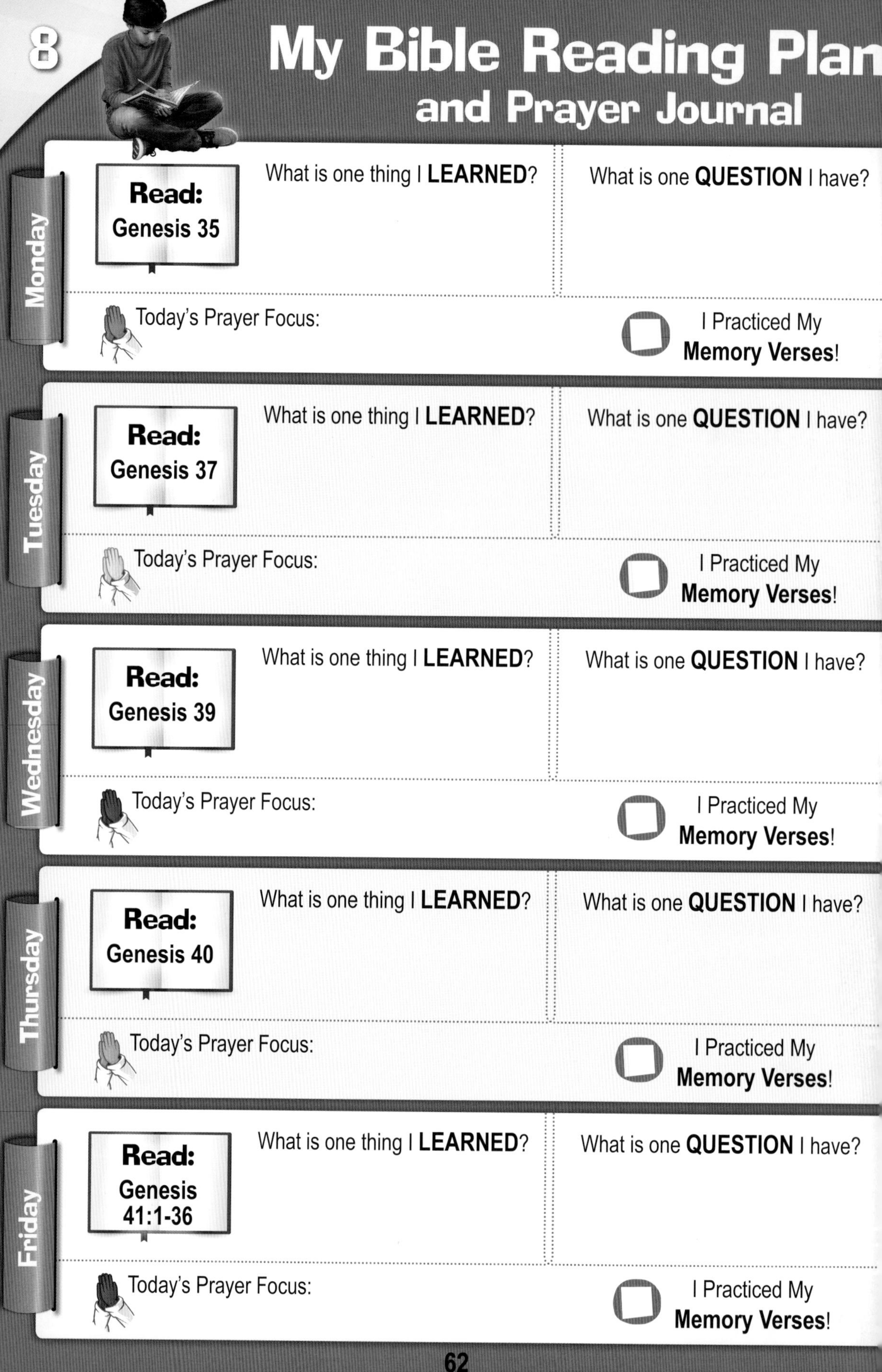

8

My Bible Reading Plan
and Prayer Journal

Monday

Read: Genesis 35

What is one thing I **LEARNED**?

What is one **QUESTION** I have?

Today's Prayer Focus:

I Practiced My **Memory Verses**!

Tuesday

Read: Genesis 37

What is one thing I **LEARNED**?

What is one **QUESTION** I have?

Today's Prayer Focus:

I Practiced My **Memory Verses**!

Wednesday

Read: Genesis 39

What is one thing I **LEARNED**?

What is one **QUESTION** I have?

Today's Prayer Focus:

I Practiced My **Memory Verses**!

Thursday

Read: Genesis 40

What is one thing I **LEARNED**?

What is one **QUESTION** I have?

Today's Prayer Focus:

I Practiced My **Memory Verses**!

Friday

Read: Genesis 41:1-36

What is one thing I **LEARNED**?

What is one **QUESTION** I have?

Today's Prayer Focus:

I Practiced My **Memory Verses**!

My Bible Reading Plan
and Prayer Journal

9

Monday

Read: Genesis 41:37-56

What is one thing I **LEARNED**?

What is one **QUESTION** I have?

Today's Prayer Focus:

I Practiced My **Memory Verses**!

Tuesday

Read: Genesis 42

What is one thing I **LEARNED**?

What is one **QUESTION** I have?

Today's Prayer Focus:

I Practiced My **Memory Verses**!

Wednesday

Read: Genesis 43

What is one thing I **LEARNED**?

What is one **QUESTION** I have?

Today's Prayer Focus:

I Practiced My **Memory Verses**!

Thursday

Read: Genesis 44

What is one thing I **LEARNED**?

What is one **QUESTION** I have?

Today's Prayer Focus:

I Practiced My **Memory Verses**!

Friday

Read: Genesis 45

What is one thing I **LEARNED**?

What is one **QUESTION** I have?

Today's Prayer Focus:

I Practiced My **Memory Verses**!

My Bible Reading Plan and Prayer Journal

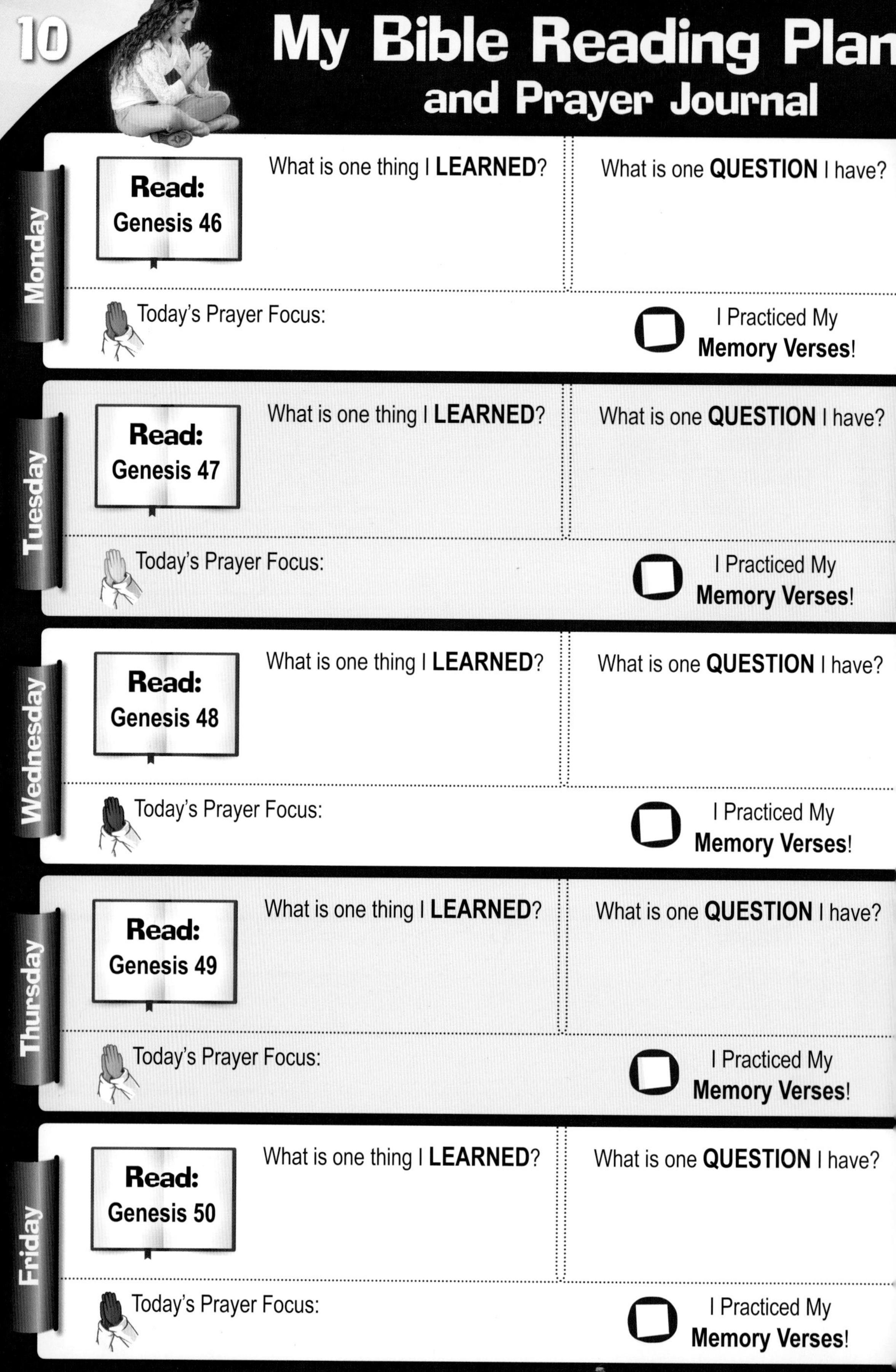

Monday

Read: Genesis 46

What is one thing I **LEARNED**?

What is one **QUESTION** I have?

Today's Prayer Focus:

☐ I Practiced My **Memory Verses**!

Tuesday

Read: Genesis 47

What is one thing I **LEARNED**?

What is one **QUESTION** I have?

Today's Prayer Focus:

☐ I Practiced My **Memory Verses**!

Wednesday

Read: Genesis 48

What is one thing I **LEARNED**?

What is one **QUESTION** I have?

Today's Prayer Focus:

☐ I Practiced My **Memory Verses**!

Thursday

Read: Genesis 49

What is one thing I **LEARNED**?

What is one **QUESTION** I have?

Today's Prayer Focus:

☐ I Practiced My **Memory Verses**!

Friday

Read: Genesis 50

What is one thing I **LEARNED**?

What is one **QUESTION** I have?

Today's Prayer Focus:

☐ I Practiced My **Memory Verses**!